The Teenager's Guide to Money

The Teenager's Guide to Money

How to Prepare for Prosperity

Empress Cindy

ECB

Empress Cindy Books, L.L.C.
empresscindybooks@yahoo.com

In memory of my parents,
refugees from the Nazis,
who taught me to love America

Table of Contents

Introduction

Right now, the American financial system is set up to benefit the wealthy, the very wealthy.

Why?

Because of the Vietnam War and the military draft.

The Vietnam War was the first one we could watch on TV, and it was extremely ugly. And the military draft meant that any healthy young man could be forced to go and fight in it.

Even worse, after the Tet Offensive in 1968, it became brutally clear that this was a war we couldn't win.

So college campuses erupted. And while most of the kids in my generation (I was born in 1950) didn't become violent, many of us did begin to seriously question the values that had gotten us into this mess and were keeping us there.

In the meantime, the people running the corporations that were making huge profits from the war started to feel threatened and decided to strike back. And since they had money and political influence and networks, they did whatever they felt was necessary to permanently regain and then increase their power.

I'm making this sound simpler than it was—as you already know, people are complex and act from a variety of motives. But as you also already know, every society has a basic power structure, and the people who have the power are not going to give it up without a fight.

So here's the bottom line when it comes to money: In America today, power=money=power, so if you want to live a prosperous life, you need to learn the rules of the system so you can be smart enough not to get sucked into financial hell.

However—and this is a *mega however*—I am not saying that you need to be rolling in money to have a prosperous life. In fact, my personal bias runs the other way. I've been alive long enough to see what a life devoted to striving for stuff can do to people, and I don't recommend it.

But—and this is a *mega but*—that is <u>your</u> decision to make. I wrote this book to give you the information you need to make the smartest choices you can to get the prosperity <u>you</u> want.

Summary

1. The American financial system is set up to benefit the wealthy, the very wealthy.

2. Power=Money=Power

3. You need to learn the rules of the financial system so you can be smart enough not to get sucked into financial hell.

Banks

There are two places where you can manage your money—banks and credit unions. And since there are a lot more banks, I'll start with them.

When you walk into a bank, you'll usually find a long counter with tellers behind it and people sitting at desks. The tellers handle your usual transactions—putting money into accounts and taking money out. The people at the desks handle everything else, like opening a checking or savings account.

I have accounts at three banks right now—I like to spread out my savings. And all the people I've met at these banks have been friendly and helpful. It's very unusual to find any other kind of folks.

But—and this matters—banks are in business to earn a profit. And the people in upper management—the CEO, president, vice-presidents, etc.—make the major decisions about how the bank operates They set policy, which means they decide how their branch banks (the buildings) work, how their online service works, how the fees and interest payments will be set, and everything else that determines how you can handle your money.

And—this *really* matters—the people in upper management get paid according to how much profit the bank makes. And since banks make their profits from us, their customers, we have to pay close attention to the rules.

I'm not going to get into the specifics of how to open an account or keep track of your spending from your checking account. The first time you go to a bank to open an account, especially if you're under eighteen, you'll have to take a parent with you. And then either your parent or the person behind the desk who helps you open an account can show you how to keep track of what you put in and take out of your account.

Instead, I'm going to give you some warnings.

First, never sign any piece of paper until you read every word on it. And if you don't understand everything you read, ask for an explanation. Your signature, once you're eighteen, is legally binding, which means that you have to live up (or down) to whatever agreement you sign. <u>So know what you're agreeing to</u>.

Second, be sure to protect your privacy. When I opened my latest savings account, I found a folded piece of paper in the folder with this question at the top: "What does Xxx Bank do with your private information?" It was followed by this statement: "Financial companies choose how they share your personal information. Federal law gives consumers the right to limit some but not all of this sharing. Federal law also requires us to tell you how we collect, share, and protect your personal information."

What kind of information can they share? Your Social Security number and income. What you do with your account and how much money you have in it. Your credit scores and specific checking account information.

Please understand that "share" often means "sell"—that's right, any company from a bank to a credit union to a car dealership that gets personal information from you from handling your money can sell chunks of your personal information. Can you say "profit"?!?

And the only kind of "sharing" you can stop is certain kinds of "marketing," which means advertising.

Still, I do call the numbers at the bottom of these forms (I also get them from my cell phone company and my credit card company) to limit as much "sharing" as I can.

Third, **never, ever** use a debit card. This is the plastic card that comes with your checking account that gives you access to the bank's ATMs (I call them automatic money machines) and that you can use in place of a credit card wherever you shop.

Why am I so fierce?

First, it's hard to keep track of all those little pieces of paper, which makes it hard to keep track of how much money you're spending.

Second, hackers can break into anything. They broke into the federal government and stole all its personnel files. They broke into the credit bureau, Equifax, and stole a lot of their financial information—including social security numbers—on most American adults. And they broke into the mega bank, JP Morgan Chase, and the bank's IT staff didn't even notice the break-in for three months.

Those card readers at all the stores where we shop are fairly easy for hackers to get into, so they can get both your debit card number and your pin and then use this information to steal from your checking account. And while each bank has a different policy, the burden of proof is on you. That means that you have to prove that thieves and not you took all that money out of your account.

Can you say "terrifying financial nightmare"?!?

Third, banks can, at any time, change their fees and rules for using a debit card.

And they do!

Finally—and this is the worst—there's overdraft protection. That's when you agree to let the bank cover any money you take out of your account after you've used up the money already in there. In other words, the bank lends you the money to cover your overdrafts.

But these loans come with a huge price! First, the bank charges you a fee for every time you use your card and need a loan, even if it's only for $1.50. And these fees range from $25 - $38 for each item. _Each item!_ Plus the bank also charges you interest, and that percentage can be very high—it depends on the bank. And if you don't put in enough money to pay for these loans and expenses within a few days, the bank will charge you even more fees and interest.

Never, ever use a debit card.

And never, ever sign up for overdraft protection.

And you also need to avoid ATM machines, because they're fairly easy to hack into. The only time I use my ATM card is when I walk into the bank and slide it through the reader on the teller counter. This reader is connected directly to the bank's computer system and is as safe as the system—I hope! I also check my checking account online at least three times a week—sometimes it pays to be paranoid.

But—and again this matters—I do not do any banking transactions online because of hackers and human error. There are a few companies that I've given access to my bank account to make bill withdrawals, but they're the electric company, the natural gas company, and the owner of my apartment complex. (I was less than thrilled about the apartment complex, but it's the only way I can pay my rent so I didn't have much choice. But I keep a very careful watch to make sure they take out the right amount, and—again—I do check my checking account online at least three times a week.)

I almost forgot—one last warning. Avoid any offers with "college" or "young adult" or any other kind of come-on. They usually assume you're inexperienced and try to take advantage of you with hidden fees.

I realize this is a lot of information to take in, especially since so much of it is negative. So let me boil it down to something simpler: Keep your financial transactions (yup, that's the fancy, technical term) as simple as possible. Do as many of them as you can in person. And be sure to read everything you sign and everything you get in the mail from your bank so you'll know what you're dealing with.

You can do this. If you pay attention to what you're doing and make sure you understand the rules, you can successfully manage your money.

Summary

1. You can manage your money at banks and credit unions.

2. Banks are in business to earn a profit. And they earn their profits from us, their customers.

3. Never sign any piece of paper until you read every word on it. And if you don't understand what you read, ask for an explanation.

4. Be sure to protect your privacy.

5. ***Never, ever use a debit card.***

6. ***Never, ever sign up for overdraft protection.***

7. Avoid ATM machines.

8. Avoid offers with "college" or "young adult" attached to them.

9. Keep your financial transactions as simple as possible. Do as many of them as you can in person. And be sure to read everything you sign and everything you get in the mail from your bank so you'll know what you're dealing with.

Credit Unions

Credit Unions are the second place where you can manage your money. They're supposed to be more user-friendly than banks, because anyone who has an account becomes a member and is supposed to have a say in how the credit union is managed.

That wasn't my experience. The people I met at the branch were as friendly and helpful as the people at a bank. But I opened a savings account with a large chunk of money and they paid a very low interest rate. When I saw that interest rates were going up at my bank, I asked if they would raise it. The woman I talked to called the chief financial officer (CFO) and he refused. So I closed my account and took my money to a bank that paid almost ten times more.

Another problem—once I joined, I would get at least one life insurance application a month with an advertising letter that was signed by the president of the credit union. That meant that the credit union was getting a nice slice off the top of every dollar the insurance company made from the members.

And I was never given the opportunity to give my opinion about how the credit union was managed.

Now, this could have been an exception to most credit unions, but I'm starting to have my doubts.

Why?

Because there are two major credit unions in my area, and last month I got a fancy card from each one that was part of a mass mailing. The first one offered a checking account with

3.03% interest. That's higher than the interest on long-term CDs! The second one offered a 5% interest rate, which is extraordinary, to put it mildly.

So I read the fine print. To get these interest rates you have to receive eStatements, instead of paper, which is fairly common. But—and this is the killer—you also have to make at least ten debit "transactions" each month for the 3.03% and at least twelve transactions for the 5%.

Can you say "overdraft charges and interest"?!?

Can you say "big bonuses for upper management"?!?

<u>Run, don't walk, away from this kind of offer</u>.

Again, this may not be happening at all credit unions, and there may be one in your area that really is more user-friendly than the banks. Just be sure you check everything out before you decide to join one.

You need to become increasingly careful with managing your money because the rules are changing so quickly. But this is in your best interest, because the more you pay attention, the more opportunities you can find to learn and get smarter.

As I said at the end of the bank chapter, I realize all this information can be overwhelming, especially since so much of it is negative. But, so what? You're smart, you're capable, and if you have the right attitude, managing your money can become one of the most exciting activities of your life.

Yee-hah!

Summary

1. Credit unions are supposed to be more user-friendly than banks but that wasn't my experience.

2. Avoid their checking accounts that pay high interest and require a large number of debit "transactions."

3. Credit unions are changing very quickly, so be sure to check everything out before you join one.

Saving

Starting today, you need to save the first ten cents of every dollar that comes into your life. What do I mean by the *first* ten cents?

I mean that you automatically take 10% of all the money that you get and immediately put it into a savings account.

If you do this, if you save 10% of all your money, you will have a solid financial future. And I'm starting with this advice because I wish someone had given it to me when I was your age—or 25 or 37!

I've always been fairly frugal, so I've never been in serious financial trouble. But if I'd started saving 10% off the top as a teenager, I would have created a financial cushion that would have made my life a whole lot easier.

This is the money you can use to pay cash for a car, pay cash for a school trip, pay cash for fancy clothes, and—most importantly—pay cash for those emergencies that always pop up in everyone's life.

Once you're out on your own, though, you're going to need to focus on building up a protection savings account (PSA) to cover your expenses for at least twelve months.

What do I mean by expenses? The money you spend in a month to keep yourself going, from rent to food to loan payments to insurance payments to gas for your car. I realize that you don't pay your insurance premiums every month, so just divide the fee by the number of months it covers so you'll know how much it costs every month.

Why do you need a PSA?

Because the only constant in the universe is change, and if you lose your job or get sick or in some other way lose your steady income, you're going to need enough money to keep living your life until you can start earning again. And since you want to fully fund this account as quickly as possible, pour in as much money as you can as often as you can.

After you've completely set up this account, you can go back to the 10% one for stuff and short-term emergencies. And you need to keep pouring in that 10% for the rest of your life.

Now let's talk about the specifics of saving beyond the 10% off the top. The simplest way is to think in terms of needs and desires.

In the U.S., most of us live in the lap of luxury. We have electricity, indoor plumbing, refrigerators, stoves, microwaves, central heat and (usually) air conditioning, roads, cars, trucks, and gas stations.

And our grocery stores! Apples in the summer, strawberries in the winter, several kinds of laundry detergent and toothpaste and soap—I could go on and on.

My point is that compared to most of the people in the world, we live like kings and queens. So we need to be really honest with ourselves when we separate our needs from our desires.

OK. We need food, a decent place to live, and clothes. If we live in an area without public transportation, we'll probably need a car or truck. We'll need a telephone, and if we're in school, probably a laptop and an internet connection.

That's it, isn't it?

We don't <u>need</u> smart phones, a zillion and one TV channels, DVDs, a DVD/Blu-ray player, or even a TV. We also don't <u>need</u> to eat out or take trips. These are all <u>desires</u> that we often convince ourselves are needs.

But when we become fiercely honest about separating the two, we start to find all sorts of ways to save money, right?

I cannot say this often enough: Our current financial system is deliberately designed to make us confuse our desires with our needs and therefore spend money we don't have on things we don't need so the people with the power can get rich from our debts.

Don't fall for it!

Don't let those bloodsuckers seduce you into getting into debt so you can buy a life that doesn't belong to you.

<u>Save your money by separating your needs from your desires</u>. And once you have enough money socked away to thoroughly take care of yourself, then—and only then—can you start fulfilling your desires in a responsible way.

Summary

1. Starting today, you need to save the first ten cents of every dollar that comes into your life.

2. Once you're out on your own, you're going to need to focus on building up a protection savings account (PSA) to cover your expenses for at least twelve months.

3. Expenses=the money you spend to keep yourself going.

4. You need a PSA because the only constant in the universe is change, and if something happens to stop you from working, you're going to need enough money to keep living your life until you can start earning again.

5. Compared to most of the people in the world, we live like kings and queens.

6. Be fiercely honest about separating your needs from your desires, because that's how you'll find all sorts of ways to save money.

7. Our current financial system is deliberately designed to make us confuse our desires with our needs and therefore spend money we don't have to buy things we don't need so the people with the power can get rich from our debts.

8. ***Don't fall for it!***

9. <u>Save your money by separating you needs from your desires</u>.

Giving

It's one thing to be frugal, but it's another to be stingy.

Why else are we here if not to make the world a better place?

And the best way to do that is to help other people.

There are three ways to donate—money, stuff, and time. For example, I used to send checks to food pantries, but I didn't like the fact that they used my money to buy food with chemical additives. So I started buying clean food and donating that instead.

As for time, I'm very upset about drive-by doctoring, which I'll explain in the chapter on health care. So I've been calling all the political candidates from my area (2018 is an election year) and talking to their staffs about it.

Giving is essential for a full life and is, in fact, the core of prosperity.

Why?

Because of the way it makes you feel.

Earning

I can guarantee that your life will not turn out the way you think it will right now.

Why?

Because the only constant in the universe is change.

When I was born in 1950, few people had televisions, telephones were wired into the wall, and what was a computer?

When I graduated from high school in 1968, the U.S. was deeply involved in the Cold War with the Soviet Union, China was isolated and a dangerous nuclear threat, and computers were gargantuan main frames. 1968 was also the year when Martin Luther King, Jr. and Robert Kennedy were assassinated, our country was being torn apart by the Vietnam War, and three heroic American astronauts orbited the moon for the first time.

As my mother used to say, who can predict the future?

And that's why it's essential that you remain open, fluid, and flexible when you think about earning money.

So let's start with the basics: <u>You need to earn enough money to pay your expenses</u>. I'll be talking about college in a little while, but the most important thing is to <u>avoid student loans</u>. They are designed to suck the blood out of you until you die.

This means that if you want to go to college you need to find a way to pay as you go.

There are two basic options for earning money—get a job or become an independent operator.

What's an independent operator?

If you've ever shoveled snow or babysat for money, you've been an independent operator.

That's right—an independent operator is simply someone who finds a way to earn money outside of a job. Fancy term, but easy to become.

There are many, many books on how to succeed in finding a job or becoming an independent operator. And when you're ready, you can go to your local library and start reading.

So I'll leave you with one last bit of advice: **Do not sell your soul for money**.

Once you start selling your integrity down the river, it is extremely difficult to get it back.

And as bad as financial hell can be, spiritual hell is even worse.

Summary

1. Who can predict the future?

2. It's essential that you remain open, fluid, and flexible when you think about earning money

3. <u>You need to earn enough money to pay your expenses.</u>

4. <u>Avoid student loans.</u> This means that if you want to go to college, you'll need to find a way to pay as you go.

5. There are two basic options for earning money—get a job or become an independent operator.

6. An independent operator=someone who finds a way to earn money outside of a job.

7. ***Do not sell your soul for money.***

8. Once you start selling your integrity down the river, it's extremely difficult to get it back.

9. And as bad as financial hell can be, spiritual hell is even worse.

College

Since I used to be a school teacher, I'm going to start by telling you the truth. The purpose of a K-12 education is not to teach you how to think, but how to behave. Like basic training in the military, it is designed to beat the independence out of you so you'll follow orders without thinking.

If you're actively fighting in a war, this training could save your life. But if you're trying to live a life with integrity and imagination, it could murder you.

Of course, K-12 is much more subtle than the military. But you've spent enough time in school to know what I'm talking about.

Another problem with K-12, especially high school, is that much of the teaching can be mediocre at best and most of what you learn is useless. And, I'm sorry to say, a college education is just the same.

There is one exception—technical classes in fields like engineering and architecture. Then you really do have to learn what the professor is teaching no matter how boring he may be. And the same rule applies to nursing, dental, medical, and law schools.

So if college is such a waste, why bother going?

For the same reason you're sticking it out in high school—the piece of paper. You need a high school diploma to get a decent job. And, in spite of our changing economy, a college degree will enable you to earn a lot more money over your lifetime.

But there is one very strong alternative—technical or trade schools. We're always going to need plumbers, electricians, auto mechanics, and repairmen. So if you're good with your hands and prefer moving around to sitting behind a desk, I strong encourage you to check this out.

You still do have to pay for these schools, so the rest of this chapter could be very helpful.

OK. The money.

Rule #1—NO LOANS.

You're going to hear again and again how student loans are the best investment you can make for yourself. And most of this advice will come from the folks who offer these loans.

Here's the problem—a student loan will stick to you like glue until you die. If you don't pay it off, the lender can take away part of your salary and even part of your Social Security! And if you miss even one payment, these lenders have all sorts of legal tricks to use that missed payment to make your loan significantly bigger.

You may have heard the term "bankruptcy." It's a legal process where people and businesses can say that they have gotten into so much financial trouble that they can't pay their debts. It's a tough process with a lot of negative side effects.

But—and this is a *huge but*—even after a person declares bankruptcy and the court clears away the debts, the student loan will still remain. That's right—you can be legally declared flat broke and the lenders can still come after you until you die.

Rule #1—NO LOANS.

So how do you pay for college or a technical school?

First, there are scholarships and grants, which give you money you don't have to pay back. There are books and websites devoted to how to find and apply for them. You can also ask your counselor.

Just be sure not to get scammed into paying for advice about scholarships and grants. There's enough information for you to do your own research.

26

Second, go to the least expensive schools you can find. That usually means starting with a community college for the first two years and then transferring to a state university.

You can also live at home, which will save you a lot of money.

Third, you can work your way through. Earn enough money for a semester or a year, and then take off as much time as you need to earn more. Yes, it could take you a lot longer to graduate, but when you do, you won't have any debts.

And that's what counts.

Now what about the fancy schools like Harvard, Yale, and Stanford?

If you live in a home where your family can afford these schools, you could be under a lot of pressure to go to one of them. So I'll tell you what I know.

The teaching won't be any better than at a state university. Why? Because professors get tenure for publishing, not teaching. (Tenure=job security.) And the fancier the school, the greater the pressure to publish, especially books, so the professors will be spending most of their time on research and writing.

These schools are also extremely hard to get into, so the competition among students can be brutal.

So why go to a wildly expensive school with distracted professors and brutal competition?

For the network.

Everyone has a network—it's your group of friends and acquaintances. And the higher up you go in society, the more important your network becomes.

Since most of the students at the fancy schools are extremely ambitious and want to make a lot of money with jobs in the upper levels of society, they can provide good connections for each other. This is especially useful if their families are already well-connected. The alumni or graduates from these schools also form a powerful network and can help students find jobs.

But you don't need to go to a fancy school to be successful and make a lot of money. You can have a good idea for a product or a service. You can open a store and then another and then another. Or you can write a book that becomes a best seller or a series of books that sells extremely well.

It all depends on what you want from life. So take some time to think about who you are and what you want.

And remember—life is full of surprises, many of them good. So remain open, fluid, and flexible, and you'll find your opportunities.

Summary

1. The purpose of a K-12 education is not to teach you how to think, but how to behave. Like basic training in the military, it is designed to beat the independence out of you so you'll follow orders without thinking.

2. Much of the teaching, especially in high school, can be mediocre at best and most of what you learn is useless.

3. A college education is just the same.

4. You go to college for the same reason you stick it out in high school—for the piece of paper.

5. Technical or trade schools are a strong alternative to college.

6. Rule #1—NO LOANS.

7. Check out scholarships and grants, live at home, go to a community college for the first two years, and keep earning the money you need.

8. Fancy schools, like Harvard, Yale, and Stanford are wildly expensive and have distracted professors.

9. The main advantage in going to them is the network you can develop.

10. You don't need a fancy school to succeed.

11. You can have a good idea for a product or a service. You can open a store and then another and then another. Or you can write a book that becomes a best seller or a series of books that sells extremely well.

Learning

More truth.

The true purpose of an education is to teach you how to love to learn.

There's nothing wrong with algebra, chemistry, or Spanish—in fact there's everything right with algebra, chemistry or Spanish—if the teacher knows how to teach, if the teacher knows how to make learning algebra, chemistry, or Spanish exciting and filled with joy.

Good teachers instinctively know that loving to learn is the only way to succeed in life. And this is especially true in our rapidly changing information economy.

So how do you learn how to love learning? Find something you love and learn everything you can about it. The world is such a fascinating place that if you open your heart and your mind, you'll always find things to love.

Do not let the education system destroy you.

Own your hearts, own your minds, and live the life that belongs to you.

Yee-hah!

Credit Cards

Avoid credit card debt.

Avoid credit card debt.

Avoid credit card debt.

OK, now let's start with the basics. First, don't get a credit card until you actually need one. As long as you can pay for everything you need with cash or a check, do it. Yes, the famous financial gurus will say that not having a credit card with hurt your credit rating (more about that in the next chapter), but until you develop strong financial discipline, credit cards can be extremely dangerous.

Eventually, you'll probably get one. If that happens, get it from your local bank.

Why?

Because there are very steep penalties for late payments, and the Post Office (USPS) is unreliable—I know this from many, many personal experiences. (That's why I pay my electric and natural gas bills directly from my checking account.) So if you get your credit card from your local bank, you can pay your bill in person in plenty of time.

How much time is plenty of time? I pay my bills as soon as I get them. So plenty of time is within three days of when you get your bill.

And this, too, can be a problem, because the USPS can also lose your bills. So I keep a small, spiral-bound calendar on my desk and I paper-clip the old bill to the page with the date when I'm supposed to receive the new one. If I don't get it within two days of that date—and this has happened—I call the number on the back of the card and find out what the bill total is. And since your card will be from your bank, you can always just walk in the door and ask either a teller or a person at a desk to find out for you.

I also use this technique to keep track of all my bills—rent, telephone, insurance, etc. I've had too many close calls because of the USPS, so I don't trust them with anything. And that's why when I have to send a quarterly tax payment to the IRS (since I get Social Security I need to do this), I always use a green card that requires a signature and comes with a tracking number. Using a green card is more expensive, but at least I can track important letters.

Back to credit cards.

Never use your credit card for anything but buying things. They offer cash advances—this is a loan, like overdraft protection, only it can last a lot longer—but the interest rate on my card is 26.74%. <u>That is outrageous</u>! They also offer balance transfers, where you can transfer the amount of money you owe on one credit card to another and they *only* charge 16.74%. Isn't that nice? That's also the interest rate when you don't pay your complete bill and have a balance left over.

16.74% is an enormous interest rate, and if you keep paying only the minimum payment that's at the top of your bill, you could take years and years to pay off the complete bill. And that's because of compound interest—you get charged interest on the interest.

There are also all sorts of rules that come with credit cards, so you have to read the information that you comes with your credit card when you first get it. Then you need to keep reading the information on both sides of your statement/bill and keep up with the changes.

Credit card companies are required by law to pay for any charges that are made by people who somehow get their hands on your number or steal your card, so they have departments that track all charges through certain computer programs. And if they think they found a false charge, they'll either call you or send an email. But if they miss a one, you have to follow *their* rules to get it taken care of, and that usually involves writing a letter.

Finally, as soon as you get your credit card, write down the card number and the phone number on the back of it. Why? Because if your card gets stolen or you lose it, you must **immediately** call that phone number and report it, so they can cancel your card number. They'll send you another card with a new number within a few days, and in the meantime you'll need to use cash and checks.

Do you see why you want to hold off on getting a credit card for as long as you can?

Credit card debt is one of the major ways the financial bloodsuckers get rich off of their customers.

Be smart.

Avoid credit card debt.

Avoid credit card debt.

Avoid credit card debt.

Summary

1. ***Avoid credit card debt.***

2. Don't get a credit card until you actually need one.

3. When you do get one, get it from your local bank so you can pay your bills early and in person.

4. Keep track of when your bill is supposed to come in the mail. If it doesn't come within two days of that date, call the number on the back of your card to find out what the bill total is.

5. <u>You cannot trust the USPS</u>, so keep track of when all your bills should arrive.

6. Never use your credit card for anything but buying things.

7. Pay attention to the rules of your credit card and the information that comes printed on your bill every month.

8. As soon as you get your card, write down the card number and the phone number on the back of it.

9. If your card gets lost or stolen, you must **immediately** call the number on the back of your card and report it, so they can cancel your card number.

10. Credit card debt is one of the major ways the financial bloodsuckers get rich off of their customers.

11. Be smart.

12. ***Avoid credit card debt.***

Credit Bureaus

Credit Bureaus exist for one reason and one reason only—to help the financial bloodsuckers make money by feeding off of the rest of us.

These credit bureaus can be very dangerous, so please pay close attention so you can learn what you need to do to protect yourself.

There are three credit bureaus—Experian, Equifax, and TransUnion. They are legally allowed to collect as much financial information about you as they can, beginning with your Social Security number. And then they issue you a credit rating, which ranges from 300-850, and the lower your rating the more the financial bloodsuckers can feed off of you.

So what kind of information do they collect? Your "personal profile," which includes your name, year of birth, address, current employer, and previous employer. They keep track of all your loans—that's right, banks, car dealerships, stores—any company that lends money just hands over all that information to these bureaus. Then the bureaus keep track of any late payments and what they call "worst current status" and "worst ever status." They also keep track of "public records," whatever that means—probably arrests, imprisonments, and definitely bankruptcies.

They also keep track of how much you owe each month. That means that if you have a car loan for $18,000, they keep track of how much you owe of that loan, including interest, each and every month. If your parents have a mortgage loan for your home, they keep track of that. They also keep track of "collection balances"—that means any accounts that have been handed over to a collection agency.

And they keep track of credit card balances. Credit cards are considered "revolving credit," which means that people have different balances every month depending on how much they spend and how much of their bills they pay. And then the bureaus compare that to the total amount of money (credit limit) each card allows them to spend. For example, let's say you have a total credit limit of $5,000, and you spent $2500 last month. The bureaus then work out the percentage you used, which would be 50%.

And then they put all this information into a computer program that figures out your score. And this program is designed to give you the lowest score possible. So the higher the percentage of credit you use, the lower your number. If you have any late payments, the lower your number. If you have any accounts handled by a collection agency, the lower your number.

And the lower your number, the more lenders will charge you for money. So if you take out a car loan, the lender will increase the percentage you have to pay in interest based on how low your credit rating is.

And it gets worse. Every time a company checks your credit rating, the credit bureau drops your score by at least four points. So let's say you're just getting started out on your own. You need an apartment and the manager checks your credit rating with one bureau. Bye-bye at least 4 points. You also need to get your own cell phone account—at least 4 more points. And cell phone companies are starting to check with all three bureaus, so you really lose at least twelve points across the board. If you take out a loan for a car, not only do you get seriously dinged for the loan, but you also get dinged when the bank or dealership checks your credit rating.

And since there are 3 bureaus, and different companies use different bureaus, you can have different scores from each one. And every time a company checks with a credit bureau it has to pay a fee, which you end up paying for one way or the other. Plus, the company can pay for a complete credit report, which means they can get all the information the bureau has collected on you.

There's more, so take a few deep breaths and prepare yourself. There's also your FICO score. It has the same range—300-850, but then there are differences. FICO only issues a score, not a full report. And according to its website, "90% of top lenders" use FICO. What are top lenders? What are middle and bottom lenders? Your guess is as good as mine.

And you'd think that because they call it a FICO <u>score</u> that there would only be one.

WRONG.

There's the overall score, and then there are the auto score, the mortgage score, and the credit card score. And then there are two levels, eight and nine.

Who can keep track of all of this? I certainly can't.

Take a few more deep breaths, because I have even more bad news. Insurance companies check our credit ratings and use them to set our fees. Is that ridiculous or is that ridiculous?!? My credit score doesn't have anything to do with the way I drive a car. What matters is my driving record. And, of course, if the insurance company checks with a credit bureau, your credit rating loses at least four points.

Plus employers are starting to check applicants' credit ratings and possibly get their entire credit reports. There's goes another ding of at least four points, not to mention a dangerous violation of the applicants' privacy.

Anyone at any time can get your credit rating, report, and/or FICO score if that person has your social security number and is willing to pay.

Anyone.

Do you see what I mean about these credit bureaus? And, if you remember from the bank chapter, hackers broke into the Equifax website and stole a lot of their financial information. So all that info is floating around the internet, all of it for sale, all of it available to use against us.

Oh—one more thing. These credit bureaus can be very sloppy in their collection of information and the way they input it into their computer systems. There's a law that says they have to correct their mistakes, but I know from personal experience that the law doesn't work unless you're willing to put in a lot of time and energy into getting that correction.

So how can you protect yourself?

AVOID DEBT.

Avoid credit card debt.

Avoid student loan debt.

Avoid car loan debt if possible.

(You're too young to have to think about a mortgage. But if the time does come, be sure you do thorough research on the bank or lending company you're using and that you borrow as little as possible.)

I realize this is all very frightening. Credit bureaus and FICO exist to help the people who pay for their information use that information to make money at our expense.

But if you're smart and if you're careful, you can manage them.

I've done a lot of thinking about our current financial system, and I've come to one conclusion: The only way to change the system is to starve it to death. And the way to starve it is to be so smart with our money that the bloodsuckers won't be able to charge us the fees and interest that make their profits.

So once again, be smart. Be careful. Don't spend money you don't have to buy things you don't need. Continue to separate your needs from your desires. Continue to save every cent you can. Build up your Protection Savings Account (PSA). Build up your 10% account. Build up your retirement account (more about this in the retirement chapter).

And avoid debt, avoid debt, avoid debt.

Summary

1. Credit bureaus exist to help the financial bloodsuckers make money by feeding off of the rest of us.

2. Credit bureaus are legally allowed to collect as much information as they can about you, beginning with your social security number.

3. They then issue you a credit rating, which ranges from 300-850, and the lower your rating the more the financial bloodsuckers can feed off of you.

4. Credit bureaus find as many ways as possible to lower your rating, because then the companies that buy your information can increase the percentage you have to pay for interest.

5. Then there's your FICO score—or rather, <u>scores</u>.

6. Insurance companies check our credit ratings and then use them to set their fees.

7. Employers are starting to check applicants' credit ratings and possibly get their entire credit reports.

8. <u>Anyone</u> at <u>any time</u> can get your credit rating, report, and/or FICO score if that person has your Social Security number and is willing to pay.

9. Credit bureaus can be very sloppy in their collection of information and the way they input it into their computer systems. And it takes a lot of time and energy to get them to correct their mistakes.

10. Protect yourself. AVOID DEBT.

Cars

Remember when talked about how banks and credit unions make outrageous profits from overdraft protection? Well, now some car dealerships have developed unscrupulous ways to increase their profits as well.

I know about this because I bought a car earlier this year. So I'll just tell you what happened.

The salesman, of course, was friendliness personified. He wasn't pushy or obnoxious, just a nice, friendly guy who liked me and wanted to give me a good deal. And I did get one.

But then the trouble started. I pay cash for my cars, so I figured all I had to do was give the salesman the certified check and sign a few forms and then my car and I could leave.

WRONG!

I first had to meet with the finance guy, who smiled and shook my hand and then took me into a small office in the back of the dealership and spent half an hour trying to terrorize me into doing things I didn't want to do.

First, he tried to scare me into getting a three-year loan for the car, with zero interest. When I said that I just paid cash, he said, "But what if your car gets totaled when you pull out of the driveway?" So I replied "I'd still have to pay back the loan, though, wouldn't I?"

Instead of answering, he then tried to terrorize me into buying up to $4,000 worth of extended protection plans that kicked in after the warranty was over. He had a computer pad, which he put in front of me and then kept sticking his hand in my face as he moved the pictures around. That's aggressive behavior, especially when a man does it to a woman.

<u>These extended protection plans are not necessary</u>. They are a strong profit center for the dealership. Any serious problems will show themselves during the warranty. And with your 10% savings account, you'll be able to cover any later repairs.

You also need to avoid getting any work done on your car at a dealership unless it's part of the warranty or a recall. Dealerships make a large chunk of their profits from their service departments. So find a good independent mechanic or a reasonably priced service franchise (a business that's part of a large chain).

Finally, when I had refused everything, he started pushing forms in front of me to sign. The first wasn't bad—"collision advantage," which "may" give me the money to cover my insurance deductible if I get in an accident.

But the second was the evil one. It's called a "Privacy Notice," but it's really a **Violation of Privacy** notice. It says that the dealership may—that "may" again—obtain information about me, and here is the kind of info: from applications, from "transactions with us, our affiliates or others," and from a "consumer reporting agency," which is a credit bureau.

Then it wants me to agree to allow them to "disclose—which means _sell_—"all of the information we collect" about me to marketing companies and financial institutions "as a consumer, customer, or former customer." In other words, they can sell my information again and again and again.

And there's more! "We may also disclose nonpublic personal information about you as a consumer, customer, or former customer to non-affiliated third parties as permitted by law." This means that they can sell my information again and again and again to anyone "permitted by law" who's willing to pay for it. And that "permitted by law" bit is so loose that it might as well not even exist.

When you get this kind of form from a car dealership or any other company, draw a huge "X" through the center and then write "**<u>NO!</u>**" in big letters at the top and the bottom on both your copy and theirs.

And, of course, that form explained why he tried to terrorize me into getting a 0% loan—he wanted all my personal information, beginning with my Social Security number, so he could sell it.

Now do you see why I'm so insistent that you read everything before you sign it?!?

I really do hate to say this, but you just can't trust anybody when there's a large chunk of money involved. It's one thing to buy groceries or even a computer. But when you start dealing with forms and credit bureaus and loans, you have to protect yourself. There are still some very good people out there, but—unfortunately, very unfortunately—they are getting crowded out by the bloodsuckers.

Be smart. Don't sign anything until you read it first. And if you don't like what it says, put an "**X**" through the center, a big "NO" at the top and the bottom, and try not to go back to that place again.

One last thing—**do not lease a car.** Leases can have all sorts of hidden charges built in, you still have to pay for all the regular maintenance, and when the lease ends you have to turn in the car.

So buy the least expensive car that fits your needs, pay as much cash as you can, and take great care of it. That way your car will last you for a very long time.

Summary

1. Some car dealerships have developed unscrupulous ways to increase their profits.

2. The salesman will be friendliness personified.

3. The dangerous man is the finance guy. BEWARE. He will try to terrorize you into buying very expensive extended protection plans.

4. DO NOT BUY THEM.

5. Avoid getting any work done on your car at a dealership unless it's part of the warranty or a recall.

6. Find a good independent mechanic or a reasonably priced service franchise (a business that's part of a large chain).

7. After the finance guy has worn you out with his terrorism, he will start shoving forms in front of you to sign. READ EVERYTHING BEFORE YOU SIGN IT.

8. Watch out for the "Privacy Notice" because it's really a **Violation of Privacy** notice. It gives the dealership your permission to sell your private information, including your social security number, again and again and again to anyone "permitted by law" who's willing to pay for it.

9. When you get this kind of form from a car dealership or any other company, draw a huge "**X**" through the center and then write "<u>**NO!**</u>" in big letters at the top and the bottom on both your copy and theirs.

10. **Do not lease a car.**

11. Buy the least expensive car that fits your needs, pay as much cash as you can, and take great care of it.

Investing

Let's start with the basics.

Investing = using your money to earn more.

A <u>stock</u>, or share, is a very small financial slice of a company.

The <u>stock market</u> is where stocks are bought and sold, or traded. It's a real place—The New York Stock Exchange (NYSE) and the Nasdaq building are both in New York City, but most trading takes place at a distance, through computers.

An <u>index</u> is a large group of stocks usually organized by the size of the companies. For example, the S&P 500 is a "large cap" index because it includes 500 of the largest companies in the U.S.

Then there are the two biggies—the <u>Dow</u> and the <u>Nasdaq</u>. The Dow contains thirty large U.S. companies chosen by the editors of *The Wall Street Journal*, which is a business newspaper. And the Nasdaq includes over 3,000 stocks ranging from technology to health care to consumer services (which is a very loose term). When you hear that the Dow opened at 25,673 and the Nasdaq closed at 6,298, those numbers are determined by mathematical formulas that depend on the price of each stock in the index.

In other words, computers have programs that figure all this stuff out, and the numbers let us know if stocks in general are going up or down. The S&P index that I talked about earlier also has opening and closing numbers. And "opening" means how much the index is worth at the start of the trading day, while "closing" means how much the index is worth at the end of the trading day.

A <u>mutual fund</u> is a group of stocks organized by a manager who wants to make as large a profit as possible. You can buy shares in a mutual fund like you buy shares in a company.

How do you buy shares in a company or a mutual fund? Through a <u>brokerage</u>, which is a business that does the buying and selling for you. And, of course, you have to pay for this service.

I'm not a trained financial advisor, so I'm going to give you the best advice I can based on my own experience. But it is *imperative*—it is *essential*—that you continue to do your own research for as long as you invest. We live in a financially volatile world, so you need to keep paying attention to what you're doing.

There are problems with the stock market.

There are problems with mutual funds.

There are problems with 401ks, 403bs, and any other employer-sponsored retirement program, which I'll talk about in the next chapter on retirement.

First the stock market.

Investing in the stock market requires knowledge, research, and continuous thought. In the 1950's, General Motors was a very strong, reliable company with a strong, reliable stock. But look at it now! If President Obama hadn't helped GM out after the 2008 crash, they would have gone belly up.

And then there's the question of integrity. Do you really want to earn money from a tobacco company that sells cancer? What about a booze company that sells alcoholism? Or a chemical company that sells Frankenfood (GMOs)?

And the question of integrity becomes even stronger with mutual funds. At least with stocks you can choose the individual ones you buy. But mutual funds are run by managers and you have no say in what they buy.

48

And then there are the fees. Oh, boy, are there fees! There's the fee to help pay the manager's salary. Then there's the brokerage fee every time the manager buys or sells a stock. Then there are all sorts of other fees with fancy names that don't tell you what they really are, because these mutual fund companies are in business to make a profit and *you* are their profit center. And, if you don't buy the fund through a retirement program, you will probably have to pay taxes. (The tax laws keep changing, so I can't give you any specifics.)

Unless you're very skilled, the research has shown that the best investment is a no-load index fund. "No-load" means the fund isn't loaded with extra fees. And an index fund buys all the stocks in a certain index, like the S&P 500.

But if the fund buys all the stocks in an index, you're stuck with *everything*, from tobacco to booze to chemicals.

Is that what you want?

And, of course you still have to pay fees for the manager's salary and the mutual fund's company's profits, although they're significantly lower than the fees for a regular mutual fund. And you also still have to pay the brokerage fee every time a stock is bought or sold. And there still could be taxes.

Plus you have to a fee to the brokerage that you use to buy the index fund. And you continue paying all these fees every time you invest.

Finally, you're still tied to the stock market's ups and downs.

There's also a new kind of fund that you can get at most banks. This fund promises you the gains of the stock market without the losses. That means that when the market goes up you earn money, and when it goes down you don't lose any.

Sounds pretty good, right?

But you have to remember that the investment banks and companies that offer these funds are in business to make a profit. So if they give you the gains and protect you from the losses, they're going to have to find another way to earn that profit.

And what is that way?

Fees, of course.

First, you have to pay a sales commission to the bank that sells you the fund. And then you'll have to pay for the fund manager's salary, the brokerage fees, and whatever other fees they decide to charge. And, if the fund isn't part of a retirement program, you could have to pay taxes.

And that's why you need to be sure that you know *precisely* how much you'll be paying in fees down to the very last cent before you decide to invest any of your money.

So if I'm less than thrilled with stocks and even less with mutual funds, what do I suggest?

Government-insured CDs.

Yes, I know they're currently earning very little interest, but you're young and interest rates will eventually go up. Plus there's the magic of compound interest, where you earn interest on your interest.

I realize that what I'm suggesting goes against of the advice of the famous financial gurus. But, as I said at the beginning, I'm talking to you from my own personal experience.

In the 1990's I did invest in the stock market and an employer-sponsored retirement program (more about this in the retirement chapter). I was very careful to protect my integrity, but eventually the instability of the market got to me, so I pulled my money out and rolled it over into individual retirement account (IRA) CDs. I lost some cash, but I more than made up for it after the crash of 2008, when my CDs were not only safe but earning 5% interest.

But—and this is a huge but—what's right for me may not be right for you. I've given you the best advice I can based on what I've learned, but I am extremely, very conservative. You may want to take more risks. You may not be as picky about your investments. And that is your choice.

My job is to tell you what I've learned; your job is to think and choose what's right for you.

Summary

1. Investing=using your money to earn more.

2. A <u>stock</u>, or share, is a very small financial slice of a company.

3. The <u>stock market</u> is where stocks are bought and sold, or traded.

4. An <u>index</u> is a large group of stocks usually organized by the size of the companies.

5. Then there are the two biggies—the <u>Dow</u> and the <u>Nasdaq</u>.

6. A <u>mutual fund</u> is a group of stocks organized by a manager who wants to make as large a profit as possible. You can buy shares in a mutual fund like you buy shares in a company.

7. You buy stocks and mutual funds through a <u>brokerage</u>, which is a business that does the buying and selling for you. And, of course, you have to pay for this service.

8. It is *imperative*—it is *essential*—that you continue to do your own research for as long as you invest.

9. There are problems with the stock market and mutual funds.

10. I'm a conservative investor so I put my money in government-insured CDs.

11. What's right for me may not be right for you, so do your own research, think, and then choose what's right for you.

Retirement

You're probably wondering why I'm including a chapter on retirement when you're still so young. It's because once you turn eighteen, you'll be bombarded by messages, mainly from advertisers, that if you don't start investing in your retirement NOW, you'll end up eating cat food because you'll need your money to pay for all your expensive medicines.

Don't believe a word of it.

And never, ever get sucked in by scare tactics.

However, the sooner you start to save for your retirement, the more time your money will have to earn more money. So why not start a retirement savings account right now and put in at least $10 a month? You can squeeze that out if you really try. And then when you get enough money to get a CD with a decent interest rate, get it and keep on saving.

Now let's get to some specifics. There are two kinds of individual retirement accounts (IRAs). The first is the traditional, where you put in pre-tax dollars and then pay taxes on everything you take out. "Pre-tax dollars" means that you can deduct the amount you put into the IRA from your income when you file your income taxes. But you can't take out any money until you're 59 ½ without paying a penalty, and, as I said, you'll have to pay income taxes on everything.

The other IRA is a Roth, where you put in post-tax dollars and don't have to pay taxes on anything. "Post-tax dollars" means that you've already paid taxes on the money you put in. And after a certain amount of time, you can take out all the money you put into the account, though not any of the extra money you've earned, without paying a penalty or taxes. And then when you turn 59 ½, you can take out that extra money as well without paying any taxes.

The Roth is a much better deal, don't you think?

Since these IRAs are controlled by the federal government, there are some very specific rules—for example, how old you have to be before you can open one, how much money you can put in within a year, and how many years you have to wait before taking money out of your Roth. But these rules change frequently so you need to check with the place where you open your account to find out what they are.

There are 3 places where you can open an IRA—a bank, a credit union, and a brokerage. With a bank or a credit union, you can open your account and handle it in person. But you are limited by what they offer. Both have CDs, and most banks have those new funds that give you the gains of the stock market without the losses. I don't know what else credit unions offer, since they're changing so quickly, so you'll have to check that out for yourself.

Since most brokerages are online, you'll need to open and handle your account through the internet. But they do offer a variety of investments—individual stocks, mutual funds, and index funds. They often offer other kinds of investments as well, but each brokerage is different, so—again—you'll have to check this out for yourself.

Now we need to talk about employer-sponsored retirement programs, primarily 401ks and 403bs. And this can get complicated, so please stay with me.

I'm going to be making an assumption here that you will be working full-time for a company that offers a retirement program. So on your first day of work, you'll be given some forms to fill out for your income tax deductions and medical insurance. You may also be given a form to sign up for the retirement program. ***Don't fill it out***—I'll explain why in a minute.

But—and this is a *gargantuan but*—there is now a law that encourages employers to automatically enroll you in the program. That's right—no one asks you what you want, they just start deducting money from your paycheck. The members of Congress who passed this law said they did it for your own good, because it would force you to save for your retirement. But we all know the truth—they did it to line the pockets of the companies that make money from these programs.

So if you do not get a form for enrollment, you **must ask** if you'll be automatically enrolled. And if they say yes, you must ask for a form that allows you to **opt out**.

Why am I so fierce about not enrolling in the retirement program?

Because once you put money into one of these programs, you'll have a very hard time getting it out until you're 59 ½. You'll have to fill out forms and then wait, and then you'll have to pay an early-withdrawal penalty plus taxes.

So this is my most important advice—**Do not invest in any employer-sponsored retirement program until you have enough money in your PSA to cover twelve months of expenses.**

Now some of the famous financial gurus insist that if your employer matches your investment, which means that for every dollar you put in, they put in a dollar up to a certain amount, you have to join the program because it's free money.

Don't buy into that.

Why?

Because you could lose your job at any time, and then how will you support yourself until you find another?

Now, let's get into the specifics of how these employer programs are run. The most important word here is—you guessed it—**fees**. These programs are administered by companies that are in business to make a profit, so they're going to charge some big fees to you just to participate. Then these programs are made up of mutual funds, which mean you'll have to pay all the fees that go with mutual funds. And, as Tony Robbins points out in *Unshakeable* (Simon & Schuster, 2017), these fees can add up to 9% of every dollar you put in! (p.64).

Each program does offer a choice of several funds, which sounds good. But, as Robbins also states, mutual fund companies are legally allowed to pay a program administrator to include their funds among the choices (p. 65). Can you say "legalized bribery"?!? And do you think these will be the most successful funds?

Things continue to get worse. Remember when I said that the best fund to buy is an index fund? Most of these programs don't offer index funds, and if they do, they find ways to add fees to make them more expensive (Robbins, p. 66).

Finally, you're still stuck with the ups and downs of the stock market. You're probably too young to remember how many people lost almost all their money in these retirement programs after the 2008 crash. As I'm writing this (October 6, 2018), the market is still doing well. But recessions are a fact of economic life. And since the people running the investment banks that caused the crash didn't have to pay for what they did, they're still making very risky deals. Why? Because they think the government and the Federal Reserve Bank will bail them out again.

Like the rest of the financial laws passed by Congress, the laws governing employee-sponsored retirement programs are designed to benefit the companies that make profits from them, not you.

Can you tell I don't like them?

But—and again this is a huge but—you still need to do your own research and make up your own mind. Again, I'm being very blunt about my prejudices so you'll know where I stand.

And now we need to talk about the huge, red-white-and-blue elephant standing in the room—Social Security. My gut feeling is that it will still be around when you retire. But the world is changing so fast that I can't be sure. So you need to be prepared to completely take care of yourself when you retire.

But—and this is a good one—research on long, healthy lives shows that people do better when they keep on working. If you end up with enough money to retire, you can either keep working for money or volunteer your time. But you really don't want to spend any part of your life just sitting around and being entertained.

Life is meant to be lived!

So make sure you create a life for yourself that's filled with interesting and meaningful activity.

Yee-hah!

Summary

1. Don't get suckered in by the scare tactics connected to retirement saving.

2. The sooner you start to save for your retirement, the more time your money will have to earn more money.

3. There are two types of retirement accounts—traditional and Roth IRAs.

4. Roth IRAs are more flexible and the better investment.

5. Be careful when you get a job and fill out the forms. There is a law that allows employers to automatically enroll their employees in a retirement program. DON'T GO ALONG WITH IT. Ask if they do this, and if they do, as for the form that allows you to *opt out*.

6. You want to wait until your protection savings account (PSA) is fully funded before you invest in a formal retirement program.

7. There are problems with employer-sponsored retirement programs, especially with the fees.

8. Do your research, think, and then decide what's right for you.

Health Care #1

The Greedos have taken over our health care system. Our Presidents and members of Congress have passed laws that enabled them to turn health care into legalized extortion.

Here's how *Merrriam Webster's Collegiate Dictionary (Tenth Edition)* defines extort: "to obtain from a person by force, intimidation, or undue or illegal power" (p. 412). The Greedos don't use force, but they do use legal intimidation and undue power.

Here's how it works. When, as an adult, you go to a place for medical care, you usually have to sign a form promising you'll pay all the bills they send you. (Even if you don't have to sign one, most places will still send a collection agency after you if you don't pay.)

This isn't that much of a problem with doctors who have offices, because they accept most insurance programs in order to get patients. (Yes, medicine is now a full-time business.) But you still have to check when you call to make an appointment to make sure they accept <u>your</u> insurance.

Even with insurance, though, you'll still have to pay substantial amounts of money on your own.

Why?

<u>Deductibles</u>=the amount you have to pay before your insurance kicks in. And they're getting bigger every year.

<u>Co-pays</u>=the amount you have to pay even after your insurance kicks in. And these are growing every year as well.

The serious trouble starts with medical facilities, places like x-ray centers, labs where they examine your blood or tissue (small bits of your body), and—especially—hospitals.

This trouble has a name—*drive-by doctoring*.

Most hospitals no longer have doctors on their staffs. Instead, they hire them with contracts. Therefore, these doctors do not have to participate in the same insurance programs as the hospitals.

And most hospitals *do insist* that you sign that form promising to pay. And most hospitals **do not** tell you that many of the doctors who work there will not accept your insurance.

So if someone has an accident and is brought into the emergency room, he or a member of his family has to sign that form. But the emergency room doctor probably won't accept his insurance. If he needs an x-ray, the radiologist who reads it probably won't accept his insurance. If he needs surgery, the anesthesiologist who gives him the drug to put him to sleep probably won't accept his insurance. Even the surgeon and/or his assistants might not accept his insurance.

And if he needs physical therapy, the therapist probably won't accept his insurance. And if his doctor sends in a social worker, psychologist, or psychiatrist, that person probably won't accept his insurance.

And none of these so-called professionals will tell him that they don't accept his insurance.

So a few weeks after he gets home, while he's still recovering, he could get medical bills for thousands of dollars that he will have to pay. And if doesn't have the money to pay them, he'll have to declare bankruptcy, which will destroy his credit rating and FICO score for at least five years.

Talk about being ambushed!

Do you see why I call this system legalized extortion?

While there are ways to deal with the finance system, there is no way around drive-by doctoring because it's legal and air-tight. So we have to change the federal law.

60

And here's the new law:

Every medical professional who works in a health care facility must participate in the same insurance programs as the facility.

A health care facility is any place where patient care is given.

This law will go into effect sixty days after it is passed.

I'll talk about how we can get this law passed in the chapter, "Power," later on.

But until we change the law, it is absolutely essential that you keep socking away as much money as you can into savings so you can protect yourself.

Summary

1. The Greedos have taken over our health care system. Our Presidents and members of Congress have passed laws that enabled them to turn health care into legalized extortion.

2. Be sure to check when you call to make an appointment with a doctor that s/he accepts <u>your</u> insurance.

3. Even with insurance, though, you'll still have to pay substantial amounts of money on your own.

4. <u>Deductibles</u>=the amount you have to pay before your insurance kicks in. And they're getting bigger every year.

5. <u>Co-pays</u>=the amount you have to pay even after your insurance kicks in. And these are growing every year as well.

6. The serious trouble starts with medical facilities, places like x-ray centers, labs where they examine your blood or tissue (small bits of your body), and—especially—hospitals.

7. This trouble has a name—*drive-by doctoring*.

8. Most hospitals *do insist* that you sign a form promising to pay any bills that they and their professionals send you. And most hospitals ***do not*** tell you that many of the doctors who work there will not accept your insurance.

9. While there are ways to deal with the finance system, there is no way around drive-by doctoring because it's legal and air-tight. So we have to change the federal law.

10. And here's the new law:

    Every medical professional who works in a health care facility must participate in the

    same insurance programs as the facility.

    A health care facility is any place where patient care is given.

    This law will go into effect sixty days after it is passed.

11. Until we change the law, it is absolutely essential that you keep socking away as much

    money as you can into savings so you can protect yourself.

Health Care #2

There are some fine doctors out there who really care about their patients. But, unfortunately, more and more doctors are putting profits before patient care.

So I wrote this chapter to help you protect yourself from them.

When you see a doctor for an exam, he's probably going to run some blood tests. He'll either take your blood in his office and then send it out to a lab to be examined or send you directly to the lab to have your blood taken there.

This is when you need to be very careful.

Why?

Because doctors can have several reasons for ordering unnecessary tests. And there's a limit to what your insurance will cover, especially with those deductibles and co-pays.

That's why before you agree to have your blood taken, you need to ask for a list of the tests and an explanation for each. If your doctor asks you why, just say you want to learn as much as you can about medicine. Then you need to make sure the lab participates in your insurance. If the doctor isn't sure, ask him to check. And if it isn't covered by your insurance, ask him to use a lab that is.

If he refuses to do any of these things, walk out the door and find a new doctor.

Remember—it's your body and your money.

Now we have to talk about prescriptions for medicine. And this can become extremely dangerous for you.

Why?

Because, according to the website, *thehealthyhomeeconomist.com*, "Doctors are making money—LOTS of money for prescribing drugs to you and your family. Chemotherapy kickbacks are the worst."

Furthermore, in 2009-2010, seven drug companies paid 17,000 doctors and 380 received more than $100,000 each.

$100,000!

Plus, "In 2009, 8/10 doctors admitted to accepting free samples, gifts, or payments from drug companies." (*thehealthyhomeeconomist.com/is-your-doctor-getting-drug-kickbacks*)

And now we come to painkillers. *All prescription pain medications can become addictive*. If your doctor prescribes one, *do not buy it until you check it out*. You can go online or use reference books from the library. And if you don't like what you find, tear up that prescription and throw it out.

And if the prescription is for an **opioid**, tear it into little pieces, throw it out, and find another doctor.

Why?

Because **opioids are extremely addictive and have destroyed thousands and thousands of people's lives**.

And people who become addicted to opioids usually turn to heroin because it's cheaper and easier to find.

AVOID OPIOIDS.

And now the teacher in me is going to take over.

Never, ever take any medicine because it's fun and makes you feel good.

All medicine can become addictive. And many heroin addicts came to heroin after popping pills.

Heroin is always, always addictive.

And heroin addicts destroy themselves and everyone around them.

So here's my list of "don'ts" for your protection:

<u>Don't have casual sex</u>.

    -- It hardens your heart.

    -- It destroys your self-respect.

    -- You could catch a sexually transmitted disease (STD).

<u>Don't drink alcohol</u>.

    -- In most states it's illegal until you're twenty-one.

    -- It harms your judgment, especially while driving.

    -- You could have the gene for alcoholism, and once you get sucked into that, it is extremely, extremely difficult to get out.

<u>Don't take illegal drugs</u>.

    --You could get arrested and sent to prison, especially if you also sell them.

    --They are always addictive and usually lead to heroin.

    --You could kill yourself with an overdose. According to Beth Macy in *Dopesick* (Little Brown and Company, 2018), in October, 2017, there were seven overdose deaths every hour (p.281).

SEVEN OVERDOSE DEATHS EVERY HOUR!!!

And please, please, do not smoke. My father was a smoker and died a very hard death from lung cancer.

I want better for you.

And I want you to want better for yourself.

Summary

1. There are some fine doctors out there who really care about their patients. But, unfortunately, more and more doctors are putting profits before patient care.

2. Doctors can have several reasons for ordering unnecessary tests. And there's a limit to what your insurance will cover, especially with those deductibles and co-pays.

3. Before you agree to have your blood taken, you need to ask for a list of the tests and an explanation for each. If your doctor asks you why, just say you want to learn as much as you can about medicine. Then you need to make sure the lab participates in your insurance. If the doctor isn't sure, ask him to check. And if it isn't covered by your insurance, ask him to use a lab that is.

   If he refuses to do any of these things, walk out the door and find a new doctor.

4. According to the website, thehealthyhomeeconomist.com, "Doctors are making money—LOTS of money for prescribing drugs to you and your family. Chemotherapy kickbacks are the worst."

5. _All prescription pain medications can become addictive_. If your doctor prescribes one, _do not buy it until you check it out_. You can go online or use reference books from the library. And if you don't like what you find, tear up that prescription and throw it out.

6. And if the prescription is for an **opioid**, tear it into little pieces, throw it out, and find another doctor.

7. **_Opioids are extremely addictive and have destroyed thousands and thousands of people's lives_.**

8. People who become addicted to opioids usually turn to heroin because it's cheaper and easier to find.

9. ***Never, ever take any medicine because it's fun and makes you feel good.***

10. All medicine can become addictive. And many heroin addicts came to heroin after popping pills.

11. ***Heroin is always, always addictive.***

12. Don't have casual sex.

13. Don't drink alcohol.

14. Don't take illegal drugs.

15. And please, please, do not smoke. My father was a smoker and died a very hard death from lung cancer.

Food

If you want to make your brain crazy and increase your risk of cancer, just keep eating food that's loaded with chemical additives.

That's right—chemical additives, all the stuff that's in your food and drinks that isn't food, make your brain crazy and increase your risk of cancer.

How do I know this?

In 1974 Dr. Ben F. Feingold published *Why Your Child Is Hyperactive*, where he proved conclusively that ADHD is caused by chemical additives (hyperactivity = ADHD). And if you look at his list of symptoms, you'll see several of the ones that are now associated with the autism spectrum.

Then, in 2014, Michio Kaku published *The Future of the Mind*, where he cited a study by Harvard Medical School and Massachusetts General Hospital that found a genetic link between ADHD and autism, depression, bipolar disorder, and schizophrenia. This gives further proof that autism is caused by chemical additives. It also explains why people who take anti-depressants can become suicidal—the pills not only have the medicine chemical, but also food coloring, binders, and possibly preservatives.

I know this is getting a bit heavy, but it's important, because more and more kids your age are suffering from "mood disorders," which is another way of saying that your brains are in trouble.

And since the 1990's there's been increasing, solid evidence linking chemical additives to cancer—just go to any search engine and type "food additives cancer," "food coloring cancer," and "preservatives cancer."

And recently there's been increasing evidence linking chemical additives to Alzheimer's.

This really is important, because when I was growing up, no one had ADHD, and even though I lived outside of Chicago, I never heard of a child getting cancer. And now, tragically, there are entire hospitals devoted to kids with cancer.

The plague of ADHD, autism, mood disorders, and cancer began to spread in the 1980's, when food companies started loading their products with chemicals. And, of course, there are the junk food places where the food can have more chemicals than actual food.

So here's my protection diet. It's going to take a lot of discipline to keep it, but I care about you and I want you to be sane and healthy, which is why I'm including this chapter. And, the fewer problems you have with your health, the less money you need to spend on health care, right?

Here are the two basics—no additives, including food coloring and natural and artificial flavors, and no chemicals, including preservatives, MSG, and artificial sweeteners.

You also need to avoid GMOs.

And, whenever possible, buy organic. Organic farming doesn't use chemical fertilizers and pesticides. This means that your food is clean from the start, and it also helps protect the water, which eventually absorbs anything that goes into the ground.

Speaking of water, tap water is dangerous. It all has lead, and when it passes through the municipal pipes to get to your home and then through your pipes to get to your faucet, it can pick up more lead, as well as other chemicals. Even worse, the chlorine that all water departments use to keep the water safe dissolves into several dangerous carcinogens (cancer-causers) when it gets into your body.

I have a filter on my kitchen sink faucet, and I also drink bottled spring water. Plus—and this does matter—I use spring water when I cook. Water gets absorbed into food when we cook it, so we need to make sure the water is clean.

Then there are animal products, from eggs to dairy to meat to fish. You have to check everything you buy, first, to make sure it hasn't been injected or sprayed with preservatives. A lot of chicken has sodium phosphate injected into it, even though the label will say "no preservatives." SP used to be listed as a preservative by the FDA (Food and Drug Administration), but somehow the companies with the money got the FDA to take it off the list. It's still a chemical, and it's still dangerous.

And most red meat is sprayed with preservatives before it leaves the packing plant. And because it's only sprayed, nothing is listed on the label.

Then you have to pay attention to what the animals ate. When you buy eggs or dairy, just get organic, so you don't have to worry about what chemicals were put into the animals' food. And buy as much organic meat as you can, of course, and if you can't find it at your grocery, then you need to go to Whole Foods or a health food store where the meat will at least be preservative-free.

Finally, when you buy deli meats, the sodium phosphate issue becomes major, because a lot of deli counters have signs that say "no preservatives" without listing the actual ingredients. Ask to read the labels, buy packaged meat that has a label, or—again—go to Whole Foods or a health food store.

Fish is another issue. Always buy "fresh caught," and even then limit how much you eat, because all our rivers, lakes, seas, and oceans are polluted.

In other words, you're going to have to become an additive detective when you go food shopping—that's right, I'm encouraging you to go with your parent(s) and participate in buying food. If you're old enough to read this book, you're old enough to take care of your health, right?

And since you want everybody in your family to be healthy, you can be a blessing to them as well.

So you're also going to have to read every single label on every single package, bottle, or can for all the ingredients. And if you find anything that isn't food, don't buy the product. You also need to be careful with toothpaste—if it has color and a sweet taste, it's probably going to have food coloring and artificial sweeteners. And then there are vitamins, which are loaded with color and binders (the stuff that holds a pill together). And if it's in a capsule, the capsule could be made out of chemicals and have coloring. The same holds true for any medicine you might take.

You're not going to have control over prescription medicines, but you do have quite a bit over the stuff you buy on the shelves, called over-the-counter medicine. I buy any vitamins or medicines I might need at Whole Foods, because they have clean alternatives. You could also try any health food stores in your area.

There's also a problem with "fortified" food, which means it contains extra vitamins—more chemicals. If you need vitamins, then take them separately, not in your food. Then you can at least control the quality.

I know this is a lot to take in, so I'll make it simple—**no chemicals**. Read every label, ask questions, and if you have any doubts, don't buy it. And then purify your drinking water and also drink and cook with bottled spring water.

Now let's move on to eating out. How much control do you have over the quality of the food you get in a restaurant? Zero, zilch, none. This is especially true with fast food joints, because the only way they can afford to give you low-priced food is by buying low-priced food and then preserving it so it lasts a long time.

Even expensive restaurants may buy some of their food from the big food companies that load their products with chemicals. And if their meat isn't organic, chances are it has been injected or sprayed with chemicals and the animals were fed with chemically laced food.

74

And that's why I never eat out. I always buy my own food and then cook it my own way. I know that can sound crazier than crazy, but I break out in hives from chemicals, I want to keep my brain sane, and I want to remain cancer-free. Plus, think of all the money I save!

So here's my big suggestion to you—become smart cooks. Learning to cook can only be an advantage when you go out into the world on your own. And boys—this isn't just for girls. Just think about the famous male chefs. Cooking can be an exciting career path. And it's a great way to make friends—who doesn't love yummy, healthy food?

Eating right could become a major problem when you go to college and live in a dorm. So you'll have to be creative and figure out what you can eat and then provide for yourself what you can't.

I realize this is all starting to sound absolutely impossible. So please take a moment to think about all the people whose health has been mangled by chemicals. There are the kids who have been labeled with ADHD and have to take those awful pills that turn them into zombies. Even worse are the kids who have been labeled with the autism spectrum and are treated like idiots and given pills that make them sicker, because the medicine and the coloring and the binders and the preservatives are all chemicals.

And then think about all the people you know who have had cancer and the misery and torture they've gone through because of it. Cancer will probably still exist even if we can get all the chemicals out of our food and drug supplies—it's a complex and complicated disease. But since we know that chemicals cause so much of it, cutting them out of our lives will definitely decrease the number of suffering people.

Although I hate to say it, this really boils down to money, doesn't it? Our food and drug supplies wouldn't be loaded with poisonous chemicals if the people doing the loading weren't making a lot of money from it, right? And remember what that website said about doctors making "LOTS of money" from chemotherapy kickbacks? And the drug companies have made so much money from ADHD medicines that I can't even give you an accurate estimate.

There really is only one way to get these chemicals out of our food and drug supplies—a quiet boycott, where we just don't buy them. All these companies, including restaurants, are in business to make money. But if they stop making money, if—in fact—they start losing money, then they'll have to change the way they do their business, right?

What's more inconvenient—providing your own, safe food or chemotherapy?

Summary

1. Chemical additives, all the stuff that's in your food and drinks that isn't food, make your brain crazy and increase your risk of cancer.

2. There is solid proof that chemical additives cause ADHD, the autism spectrum, depression, bipolar disorder, and schizophrenia.

3. There is solid proof that chemical additives cause cancer—just go to any search engine and type "food additives cancer," "food coloring cancer," and "preservatives cancer."

4. Here are the two basics of my protection diet—no additives, including food coloring and natural and artificial flavors, and no chemicals, including preservatives, MSG, and artificial sweeteners.

5. You also need to avoid GMOs.

6. Whenever possible, buy organic. Organic farming doesn't use chemical fertilizers and pesticides. This means that your food is clean from the start, and it also helps protect the water, which eventually absorbs anything that goes into the ground.

7. Tap water is dangerous.

8. I have a filter on my kitchen sink faucet, and I also drink bottled spring water. Plus—and this does matter—I use spring water when I cook. Water gets absorbed into food when we cook it, so we need to make sure the water is clean.

9. You have to check the every animal product you buy, from eggs to dairy to meat to fish, first, to make sure it hasn't been injected or sprayed with preservatives. A lot of chicken has sodium phosphate injected into it, even though the label will say "no preservatives." SP used to be listed as a preservative by the FDA (Food and Drug Administration), but

somehow the companies with the money got the FDA to take it off the list. It's still a chemical, and it's still dangerous.

10. You have to pay attention to what the animals ate. When you buy eggs or dairy, just get organic, so you don't have to worry about what chemicals were put into the animals' food. And buy as much organic meat as you can, of course, and if you can't find it at your grocery, then you need to go to Whole Foods or a health food store where the meat will at least be preservative-free.

11. Always buy "fresh caught" fish, and even then limit how much you eat, because all our rivers, lakes, seas, and oceans are polluted.

12. You're going to have to become an additive detective when you go food shopping—that's right, I'm encouraging you to go with your parent(s) and participate in buying food.

13. You're also going to have to read every single label on every single package, bottle, or can for all the ingredients. And if you find anything that isn't food, don't buy the product.

14. You also need to be careful with toothpaste—if it has color and a sweet taste, it's probably going to have food coloring and artificial sweeteners. And then there are vitamins, which are loaded with color and binders (the stuff that holds a pill together). And if it's in a capsule, the capsule could be made out of chemicals and have coloring. The same holds true for any medicine you might take.

15. You're not going to have control over prescription medicines, but you do have quite a bit over the stuff you buy on the shelves, called over-the-counter medicine. I buy any vitamins or medicines I might need at Whole Foods, because they have clean alternatives. You could also try any health food stores in your area.

16. There's also a problem with "fortified" food, which means it contains extra vitamins—more chemicals. If you need vitamins, then take them separately, not in your food. Then you can at least control the quality.

17. How much control do you have over the quality of the food you get in a restaurant? Zero, zilch, none.

18. I never eat out. I always buy my own food and then cook it my own way. I know that can sound crazier than crazy, but I break out in hives from chemicals, I want to keep my brain sane, and I want to remain cancer-free. Plus, think of all the money I save!

19. Become smart cooks. Learning to cook can only be an advantage when you go out into the world on your own.

20. Eating right could become a major problem when you go to college and live in a dorm. So you'll have to be creative and figure out what you can eat and then provide for yourself what you can't.

21. I realize this is all starting to sound absolutely impossible.

22. What's more inconvenient—providing your own, safe food or chemotherapy?

Privacy

I don't do social media because I think it's dangerous.

Why?

For starters, because it's designed to be emotionally addictive. In *The Coddling of the American Mind* (Penguin, 2018), Greg Lukianoff and Jonathan Haidt include a statement from Sean Parker, the first president of Facebook, where he admits that they designed it to "consume as much of your time and conscious attention as possible." He also says that they wanted to "give you a little dopamine hit every once in a while…" (p. 147)

Dopamine is a chemical that your brain releases that gives you a natural high. In small doses it's delightful. But if you overdo it, your brain will become addicted and push you to do whatever it takes to keep giving it more and more and more.

Anger, especially rage, is also extremely addictive, and social media excels at provoking it.

Is this how you want to live your life, as an emotional addict?

Social media also has serious problems with privacy. First, thanks to the Patriot Act, the National Security Agency (NSA) can monitor everything you do online. Everything.

Second, the companies that own the sites also monitor everything you post.

Why?

Because they're in business to make money. And since they provide the service for free, they have to find another way. So they collect as much information as they can about you and then use it to make money, primarily through advertising.

Third, more and more employers are insisting that you give them access to your Facebook page before they'll hire you. And if they do hire you, they'll insist on keeping that access. And if you post something they don't like, you're out.

Fourth, predators will try to worm their way into your confidence by taking on a false identity.

And, fifth, hackers can break into anything and use the information they get however they want.

Is this how you want to live your life, constantly being spied upon?

You're also constantly monitored if you use a free email account. The providers have programs that read every email that comes in and goes out and then use the information to target you for specific advertising.

And if you use Google as a search engine, you are constantly tracked, again to target advertising. That's why I use *duckduckgo.com*, because they don't track me.

Everything you do when you connect to the internet or other people is monitored.

When your cell phone is on, you're tracked by the power stations that transmit calls. The NSA can also track your cell phone use. And, believe it or not, some stores now have the capability to track you the minute you walk in the door.

That's why it is so important that you ***do not sext***, because someone, somewhere will have an easy time finding and looking at your pictures.

It's also illegal to sext if you're under 18. That means that you can be investigated and arrested, which happened to a group of kids in my part of the country.

Finally, sexting is self-destructive. Your body is a gift, the home you live in, and you need to treat it with respect.

I wrote this chapter because I want you to think. I want you to think about what you do on social media. I want you to think about what you do online. And I want you to think about what you do with your cell phones.

82

And now I have a particularly important warning for girls and young women. In *Coddling*, Luykianoff and Haidt talk about a book by Jean Twenge, who's a social psychologist at San Diego University, called *iGen* (Atria, 2017). She studied the frightening rise in depression, anxiety, suicide, and attempted suicide among girls and young women and found that using a smart phone, tablet, or computer, which connects them to social media, was a major cause, along with watching TV (pp. 149,152).

Please listen to me about this. I have dealt with depression myself, and it can be a very female attack.

Why?

Because females are hardwired—genetically disposed—to be more socially connected than males. Plus—and this is ***enormous***—we are indoctrinated, we are brainwashed from the very beginning to be nice, to get along with people, and to judge ourselves by the way others judge us.

Do not get sucked into this.

Yes, you want to be pleasant to people, yes, you want to get along with them, and yes, you want them to like you. But you have to be extremely very careful not to diminish your soul. If you have to choose between your soul and being popular, always, always, always choose your soul. Popularity, especially in high school, can be very costly and very, very short-lived.

Social media is extremely, extremely, extremely dangerous for females because it highlights all the ways we can be left out of things and it highlights how we are less perfect than everybody else.

And—AND—it leaves you wide open to vicious attacks, doesn't it?

Yes, there can be some good from social media, but so what? What matters is how terrifyingly dangerous it is.

You have a moral obligation to protect yourself, and the best way to do that is to think before you act.

Summary

1. I don't do social media because I think it's dangerous.

2. It's designed to be emotionally addictive.

3. Social media also has serious problems with privacy.

4. The National Security Agency (NSA) can monitor everything you do online. Everything.

5. The companies that own the sites also monitor everything you post. They collect as much information as they can about you and then use it to make money, primarily through advertising.

6. More and more employers are insisting that you give them access to your Facebook page before they'll hire you. And if they do hire you, they'll insist on keeping that access. And if you post something they don't like, you're out.

7. Predators will try to worm their way into your confidence by taking on a false identity.

8. Hackers can break into anything and use the information they get however they want.

9. Everything you do when you connect to the internet or other people is monitored.

10. When your cell phone is on, you're tracked by the power stations that transmit calls. The NSA can also track your cell phone use. And, believe it or not, some stores now have the capability to track you the minute you walk in the door.

11. That's why it is so important that you **do not sext**, because someone, somewhere will have an easy time finding and looking at your pictures.

12. It's also illegal to sext if you're under 18. That means that you can be investigated and arrested, which happened to a group of kids in my part of the country.

13. Finally, sexting is self-destructive. Your body is a gift, the home you live in, and you need to treat it with respect.

14. I wrote this chapter because I want you to think. I want you to think about what you do on social media. I want you to think about what you do online. And I want you to think about what you do with your cell phones.

15. And now I have a particularly important warning for girls and young women.

16. Depression can be a very female attack.

17. Females are hardwired—genetically disposed—to be more socially connected than males. Plus—and this is *enormous*—we are indoctrinated, we are brainwashed from the very beginning to be nice, to get along with people, and to judge ourselves by the way others judge us.

18. ***Do not get sucked into this.***

19. If you have to choose between your soul and being popular, always, always, always choose your soul. Popularity, especially in high school, can be very costly and very, very short-lived.

20. Social media is extremely, extremely, extremely dangerous for females because it highlights all the ways we can be left out of things and it highlights how we are less perfect than everybody else.

21. And—AND—it leaves you wide open to vicious attacks, doesn't it?

22. Yes, there can be some good from social media, but so what? What matters is how terrifyingly dangerous it is.

23. You have a moral obligation to protect yourself, and the best way to do that is to think before you act.

Boredom

If you are so bored that you need to engage in self-destructive behaviors like sexting, casual sex, drinking, smoking, or taking drugs, then _you need to get a life_.

Find a job, volunteer, write a book—just do something that will fill your time with meaningful activity.

Boredom is death.

It will eat into your soul like battery acid.

Get a life.

Middle Class

Just what is—or what *was*—the middle class?

I was born in 1950 and grew up in a middle-class home. At that time, middle class meant that people could afford a nice (not fancy) house and good health care without getting into dangerous debt. They were also able to help their children pay for college and sock away money for their retirement.

How many families can do that today on less than $100,000/year?!?

Of course, we also lived differently. We didn't have large closets bulging with clothes or a gazillion and one toys. Most families also had one car, a mid-priced American—there were no Japanese imports then—that they kept until it died.

We weren't surrounded with fast-food joints and only went out for dinner on special occasions. And we didn't have today's technologies—no cable/satellite TV, no laptops and tablets, and no smart phones. And, of course, no internet.

And it's because I grew up in such a different economic culture that I can have some perspective on what's going on today. Yes, we need to participate in much of our current technology. But—BUT—we don't have to go into debt or compromise our savings plan to do it. Pay for what you need, and then wait until you have all your savings set up before you buy what you desire.

Why am I being so fierce about saving?

Because stuff happens. People can lose their jobs or go through business losses. They can get seriously ill and stuck with huge medical bills. And they can get into accidents and become disabled.

I'm not saying this to scare you but to prepare you. When I was in high school, my father suffered a major business loss and a heart attack. (Yes, in hindsight, I think the two were connected.) And if I hadn't won a full tuition scholarship, I would've had a very hard time paying for college.

My mother died of cancer when she was fifty-three, and it was very expensive.

My father lived to be eighty-nine, but he needed constant care for his last eight months. And when he ran out of money he died, even though I had told him that I'd help him out.

Be smart.

Don't get seduced by frivolities.

Start saving today so you'll be able to take care of yourself tomorrow.

Summary

1. When I was born in 1950, middle class meant that people could afford a nice (not fancy) house and good health care without getting into dangerous debt. They were also able to help their children pay for college and sock away money for their retirement.

2. How many families can do that today on less than $100,000/year?!?

3. Yes, we need to participate in much of our current technology. But—BUT—we don't have to go into debt or compromise our savings plan to do it.

4. Pay for what you need, and then wait until you have all your savings set up before you buy what you desire.

5. Stuff happens. People can lose their jobs or go through business losses. They can get seriously ill and stuck with huge medical bills. And they can get into accidents and become disabled.

6. I'm not saying this to scare you but to prepare you.

7. Be smart. Don't get seduced by frivolities. Start saving today so you'll be able to take care of yourself tomorrow.

Power

When you turn eighteen you will be entering a very different world than the one I faced in 1968.

At that time there were two major power struggles—civil rights and the Vietnam War. The civil rights struggle turned out right, with enough laws on the books so Barack Obama could become president and Oprah Winfrey could become one of the wealthiest women in the world. But the struggle over Vietnam turned into a horrific, ugly, and disastrous mess that still haunts many of us who remember it.

You, however, are stepping into a very different power struggle, one that is almost as old as humankind. This is the one where the very wealthy do everything they can to get as much money as possible so they can control everybody else.

But what about the wealthy people who donate all that money to help others? Some of them could be the exception. But we still need to ask two questions: How did they earn all that money? And do they ask the people they're trying to help what they need or want, or do they use their money to tell them what to do and how to do it?

There are all sorts of ways to control.

And what makes things even worse is that most of the news media has become corrupt. During the 2016 election, I couldn't find a single honest report about Donald Trump. The writers (I can no longer call them journalists or even reporters) would take a few sentences out a speech he gave and twist them to make him sound stupid and evil.

I know this happened because I spent time digging until I found the actual speeches. And whether or not I agreed with what he said, at least I read his actual words.

Hilary Clinton was treated very differently.

We are living in very dangerous times when once-great newspapers start twisting the news.

When I was an English teacher, I used to warn my students not to believer everything they read just because it was printed in black and white. (This was before the internet.) And this warning is far more important now because we are bombarded with so much noise from so many places.

I truly believe we Americans are at a crossroads. We can continue to let the powerful use their money to own our political system or we can decide to take back our country.

I'm not talking about violent riots or even peaceful demonstrations. They don't work. Peaceful demonstrations didn't stop the Vietnam War, and while they did help the Civil Rights Movement, that was during a time when people in the media still had a sense of honor.

What we need to do is use our numbers to make the political system work *for* us.

How?

Let's start with a specific issue—drive-by doctoring, which I explained in the first chapter on health care. What we need is my three-sentence law, which I'll repeat:

Every medical professional who works in a health care facility must participate in the same insurance programs as the facility.

A health care facility is any place where patient care is given.

This law will take effect sixty days after it is passed.

So we start by bombarding our congressional representatives, senators, and the President with emails, phone calls, and snail mail, insisting that they pass the law <u>without any changes</u>. Then we add that if they don't pass this law we will vote them out of office.

And if they ignore us, we'll get rid of them by voting against every incumbent in the next election from the President on down. And we'll do that by voting for someone else.

And we'll keep on voting out the incumbents until we get this law passed.

I call this one-issue politics.

And then we'll move to the next issue, the reinstatement of the Glass-Steagall Act. This act was passed in 1933, during the Great Depression, and it separated commercial from investment banking. That means that the banks where we deposit our money must be separate from the banks that make the kind of dangerous investments that caused the 2008 crash.

And that means that if these investment banks go belly up, they won't endanger our whole economy. And that means that the President and Congress won't use our tax dollars to bail them out.

Unfortunately, it was repealed by another act in 1999, and that's one of the main reasons our economy went ka-boom in 2008.

Drive-by doctoring and the repeal of the Glass-Steagall Act are the two biggest ways the health care and finance systems are sucking our blood. There will be other issues, especially the problems with the drug companies. But once we make it clear that we will no longer allow our elected representatives to sell us down the river to line their own pockets, we'll have an easier time dealing the other issues.

Someone once said that evil flourishes when good people stand by and do nothing.

It is time for us to stop standing by and doing nothing.

It is time for us to take back our country.

Yee-hah!

Summary

1. You are stepping into a power struggle that is almost as old as humankind. This is the one where the very wealthy do everything they can to get as much money as possible so they can control everybody else.

2. Most of the news media has become corrupt.

3. We are living in very dangerous times when once-great newspapers start twisting the news.

4. We Americans are at a crossroads. We can continue to let the powerful use their money to own our political system or we can decide to take back our country.

5. We need to use our numbers to make the political system work *for* us.

6. Someone once said that evil flourishes when good people stand by and do nothing.

7. It is time for us to stop standing by and doing nothing.

8. It is time for us to take back our country.

Prosperity

So what is prosperity?

Prosperity is financial confidence.

Prosperity is knowing that no matter what happens, you have the money to take care of it.

Life is full of surprises, both good and bad. And the more you prepare for the bad ones, the more you can enjoy the good ones.

And now, since I used to be a teacher, I'm going to give you my most important advice:

Live a life that gives you the room to grow into your true, full self.

Live a life where you can get up in the morning and look in the mirror and know that your integrity is intact.

Live a life filled with work and activities that benefit humankind.

Live a generous life, because it heals your heart.

Live a meaningful life, so you can wake up in the morning with a powerful sense of purpose and go to sleep at night with a strong sense of satisfaction.

Live a soulful life, where people are more important than things.

Live a life that is worthy of you.

Conclusion

I want to congratulate the members of Congress over the past thirty-five years for the trashing of America.

Between their disastrous finance legislation and their disastrous health care legislation, they vaporized the middle class.

It is gone.

They turned the United States into a banana republic with credit cards, and that is why I decided to write this book.

Appendix

The Law of Creation

How to Get What You Want

Part I

Make a list of everything you want, from improving your health to earning more money to finding true love.

Choose the top ten.

Rank them from 1-10, with 1 being the most important and 10 the least.

Re-write them as affirmations of gratitude. For example, "Thank you, thank you, thank you for my perfectly healthy back."

Speak them aloud again and again and again.

Write them aloud again and again and again.

Keep speaking and writing until you succeed.

As soon as you accomplish one affirmation replace it with another one and keep speaking and writing.

You're going to start getting ideas for how to accomplish your affirmations. **Follow through on them**. Action is the only way to succeed.

Part II

Make a list of all the ways you can be of service to others.

Choose the top 10.

Rank them from 1-10, with 1 being the most important and 10 the least.

Re-write them as gratitude affirmations.

This is an *action list*, so take action! Perform each service. And if it's an ongoing service, continue to perform it.

As soon as you accomplish one affirmation, replace it with another one and keep taking action.

Once you figure out which are the ongoing services and which are the one-timers, make two separate lists. That way you'll have both long-term and short-term successes.

You'll find that serving others will not only increase your income and opportunities, but it will also increase your joy.

Part III

Celebrate yourself and your life by Writing Joy.

Every night write down all the good things that happened.

If you do this for ten nights straight, you'll have a new mind. All the annoyances, even all the problems, will flake away because you know that at the end of the day you'll have the very great pleasure of remembering and writing down the good stuff.

Conclusion

Success and happiness are really a result of how we think. Our minds control not only our bodies but also our lives.

So train your mind for accomplishment, train your mind for joy.

I can guarantee you, from my own personal experience, that if you put all your passion behind these three activities, **you will succeed**.

One final note: You need to be very careful with what you want. Power is neutral and can be used for good or evil. So be sure to use your power for the good.

The Law of Creation

I live my present and create my future!

Yee-hah!!!

Sources:

Byrne, Rhonda. *The Magic*. New York: Atria Books, 2012.

_____. *The Secret* (DVD). Australia (?): T.S. Productions, LLC, 2006.

Lapin, Rabbi Daniel. *Business Secrets From the Bible*. Hoboken, New Jersey: John Wiley & Sons, Inc. 2014.

Osteen, Joel. *You Can, You Will*. New York: FaithWords, 2014.

Peale, Norman Vincent. *The Power of Positive Thinking*. New York: Fireside Books, 1951, 1956, 1980.

RHJ. *It Works*. Camarillo, CA: DeVorss & Company, 1926, 1953.

Important Note: "The Law of Creation" (and **only** "The Law of Creation") is copyright-free. So you're welcome to make as many copies as you like for yourself and your family and friends and acquaintances and anyone else who might find it useful. At the risk of sounding both grandiose and naïve, I think this process could change the world.

Double Yee-hah!!!

Just For Fun

Empress Cindy's Guide to Really, Truly Easy Weaving

Introduction

I wrote this article because I love to weave, but I don't have the time or the room for big and fancy looms. So I read a lot of books about off-loom weaving, and I experimented a lot, and I came up with the method I'm writing about here.

I owe a tremendous debt to the fiber artists of Hippiedom. These folks stretched the well-honored traditions of fiber work and developed methods of working that were basic and easy and great fun. I never would have considered weaving if I hadn't seen their splendiferous work in the books and magazines of that period.

The cardboard loom I use is as basic as I can get. I also use one commercial loom quite a bit, the Peg Loom from Harrisville, which is made for children 5-7 years old. It's just perfect for me, small (6"x9") and compact and very easy to use. The easiest way to find this loom is to go online and type "peg loom" into any search engine.

I hope you'll find the satisfaction and enjoyment in weaving that have enriched my life. Most of all, I hope you'll have fun.

The Basics

You need to know only two words to weave: warp and weft. The warp is the group of vertical threads that form the backbone of the weaving. The weft is the group of horizontal threads that you weave in over and under. "Warp" can also be used as a verb to describe the process of wrapping the vertical threads around the loom.

I use the most basic weave, called plain or tabby weave. It's the over-one-and-under-one that you may have used weaving potholders or darning.

That's it! I told you this would be really easy!

Making Your Loom

The easiest way to make a loom is to use a piece of sturdy cardboard. I used to use the back of a pad of art paper, but then I found matte board. You can go to an art store and ask someone to cut up a full-sized board into whatever size pieces you want.

I find it easier to work vertically, so this time around you'll be using the cardboard with the short sides at the top and bottom. Get a ruler, hold it near the bottom edge, and leave1/2" at the end. Then mark every 1/4" until you get to the other end, and leave another 1/2". Then turn the board around and do the same thing for the other side. Don't worry about making your marks absolutely precise—yarn is very forgiving and being a little off here and there won't matter.

Now you're going to cut slits where you've made your marks. If you want your slits to be even, draw a line across the top and bottom, 1/2" from the edge. If you're using decent cardboard, it will be too thick to cut with the tips of your scissors, so try cutting it with the part of the blades down near the handles. If you're still having a hard time, try a pair of craft scissors or wire cutters or a razor-blade (utility) knife.

Take your time cutting the slits, but—again—don't worry if they're slightly off.

Now you've made your loom. Pretty easy, eh?

A Word about Frustration

Some people are better with their hands than others, and some, like me, have days when their coordination is less than thrilling. Also, though I think I've written very clear instructions, you may not agree.

So don't give up. Chances are you'll have some problems here and there—I know I certainly did—but weaving is so much fun that I didn't let my frustrations stop me.

One last thing—I'm right-handed, so I like to start working on the right side of my loom. If you're left-handed, chances are you'll find it easier to work from the left, so just alter my instructions to suit yourself.

Warping Your Loom

First, let's talk about yarn. I use all sorts of yarn, but I always enjoy the cheap, wiry acrylics. Not only are they inexpensive, but they come in a wide range of brazen colors and are sturdy and slightly elastic. This time around, you want to use a medium-sized (worsted weight) yarn that's fairly sturdy and not fuzzy. Wool would do nicely, but if you're just trying this out, why not go the cheap route? (Of course, if you already have a stash, just pull out whatever sturdy, worsted yarn you like.)

Warping is amazingly easy. Take the end of your yarn and put it into the upper, left-hand slot, leaving the end of an inch or two facing you. You're going to warp starting in the back so you'll have enough yarn for the fringe. Wrap the yarn firmly around the back and insert it into the first left-hand slot on the bottom. Then bring it up the front, again with a firm tension, and slide it into the same first slot that you put the end in. Keep wrapping the yarn firmly around the cardboard, placing it in each slot as you go. When you finish, turn the cardboard over and cut the yarn more than half-way down the loom—you're doing this so you'll have enough yarn for the fringe. Then tuck the end into some of the warp yarns to keep it safe and out of your way.

Finally, turn the cardboard back to the front and gently bend each end towards you. The key is *gently*. You're not trying to fold the board in half, but to create a little concave curve, which will make weaving easier.

That's it! You have now successfully warped your loom!

Weaving

Now you're just about ready to begin. But first a word about supplies. You need a pair of scissors that cuts yarn easily. You also need a needle or two. Right now my favorite needles are a pair of the needles knitters use to sew their knitting together, the ones with the bent points. I like the bend, because it makes it easier for me to lift the warp when I weave my yarn under it. And since these needles are made for yarn, the eyes are big enough to thread the yarn without shredding it.

Speaking of yarn...since this is your first weaving, you can use what you have around your home—stash leftovers are always a delight. Or, again, you can buy some cheap acrylics. The point is to experiment and see if you like weaving. If you do, you can invest in a wider range of yarns. I find it easiest to work in stripes, and for starting out, I think you will too. So get three or four different colors (and textures, if you'd like) that you think will work out well together.

Finally, a few words about ends. If you decide to become a serious weaver (I put myself in the slightly frivolous class), you'll need to find a way to work in the ends of your weft yarns. I find it easiest to leave the ends on the front, because pushing them between the weaving and the cardboard is annoying. I've also recently started making the ends part of my weaving design, so I use nice, long ends that create a lively fringe effect.

O.K. Now you're ready to begin. Cut a piece of yarn about three times the width of your loom and thread it into the needle. Weavers usually work from the bottom up, because that makes it easier to pack down the yarn. So you're going to start from the lower right corner.

110

Count three warp threads into the loom and weave from left to right, about an inch from the bottom. Start by going under, then over, then under.

Congratulations! You've just woven in your starting end.

The object in plain weave, which is what you're doing, is to alternate over and under on each row. Since you ended your row by going under, you're going to start your next row by going over. But because you just wove in your starting end, you're going to start your next row *below* that row. So start going over and under and over and under until you reach the left end of your loom. Smoosh the yarn down to the bottom with your fingers and weave back to the right. You'll notice that the last three under-and-overs will match the starting end. Don't worry about it—it's in the bottom corner and no one will notice.

Now all you have to do is keep weaving until you're finished, smooshing down each row as you weave it. When you reach the end of a piece of yarn, stop with an under and leave the end on the top. Start the next piece in the same place you stopped, with an under, and keep on weaving.

I've found that it's too hard to weave the last rows near the top—it's tight and I don't get good tension. So when I'm about half-way up the weaving, I turn my loom around and start with the top as the bottom. That way the tight rows come in the middle of the weaving, and they're much easier to work. You have to do a little thinking ahead, but since you're weaving stripes, you'll be able to figure things out.

That's it! You're weaving!

Finishing Your Weaving

You've finished your first weaving! Congratulate yourself. Dance to your favorite piece of music. Write "I am a weaver" in every different pen and pencil you have.

Now comes finishing. You're going to use the yarn on the back of your loom to make fringe. Turn your loom over and cut the yarn about a fourth of the way down from the top. You can either guestimate or use a ruler to measure the same distance from the top on both sides and make little marks to guide your cutting.

Now turn your loom over to the front. You're going to have a loose end where you started, and the last fringe will be too long, but you can trim that when you're done. Hold the loom so that the slits and fringe are on your right and left. Beginning in the lower right-hand corner, gently lift up the bottom two fringes and tie them together with an overhand knot (the kind you put at the end of sewing thread) as close to the weaving as you can get it. Don't worry if you don't get close enough right away—just untie the knot, using a needle to loosen it, and try again. Keep doing this up the side, knotting two fringes at a time. When you get near the top, if you have five fringes left, tie three together and then two.

Do the same thing to the other side.

That's it. Your weaving is finished. Are you a genius or what?!?

What Now?

You are now officially a weaver.

But what happens next?

I think of my weavings as yarn sketches. I like to play with color and texture and see what turns out. I call all my weavings experiments, because I don't do much planning ahead of time, except to choose the yarns I want to work with. Even then, I often change my mind and add and subtract as the work progresses.

So go to your library. I especially like the weaving books in the children's department, because the directions are usually very clear. But don't skip the adult books, because they'll have some wonderfully inspiring pictures and will lead you in more sophisticated directions. And don't go just to the weaving books—I love looking at all sorts of fiber books. And the art books— oooh, the art books! Georgia O'Keefe's watercolor, "Pink and Green Mountain," has been the inspiration for a number of my fiber pieces.

And then there are bookstores and online bookstores and mail order companies and used bookstores and library book sales and museum exhibitions and fiber guilds and craft fairs and blogs and…

I've found weaving to be a never-ending source of fun and satisfaction and excitement, and it has led me to all sorts of areas I'd never thought about before. I've joined computer lists about weaving, written on computer talk pages, joined guilds and other fiber groups, read books and magazines, and seen live fiber pieces that I didn't even know about a few years ago.

If you've enjoyed making your first loom and weaving, you have a wondrous and thrilling time ahead of you.

Suggested Books

Dendel, Esther Warner. *Needleweaving…Easy as Embroidery*. Philadelphia: Countryside Press, 1971, 1972.

Meilach, Dona Z., and Snow, Lee Erlin. *Weaving Off-Loom*. Chicago: Henry Regnery Company, 1973.

Rainey, Sarita R. *Weaving Without a Loom*. Worcester, MA: Davis Publications Inc., 2007.

And now I can't resist:

Yee-hah!

Yee-hah!!

Yee-hah!!!

About the Author

Empress Cindy is a former teacher who started publishing online in 1993. She published 102 articles on *Yahoo! Voices*, and in 2015 she published the book, *Living with ADHD/Autism, Living Without Drugs.*

You can reach her through her publisher: empresscindybooks@yahoo.com.